FROM SHAME TO FREEDOM

The Parental Guide
to Encouragement

Monique Brewer

TRILOGY

Trilogy Christian Publishers

A Wholly Owned Subsidiary of Trinity Broadcasting Network

2442 Michelle Drive

Tustin, CA 92780

For information, address Trilogy Christian Publishing

Rights Department, 2442 Michelle Drive, Tustin, Ca 92780.

Trilogy Christian Publishing/ TBN and colophon are trademarks of Trinity Broadcasting Network.

For information about special discounts for bulk purchases, please contact Trilogy Christian Publishing.

Trilogy Disclaimer: The views and content expressed in this book are those of the author and may not necessarily reflect the views and doctrine of Trilogy Christian Publishing or the Trinity Broadcasting Network.

10 9 8 7 6 5 4 3 2 1

Library of Congress Cataloging-in-Publication Data is available.

ISBN 979-8-89041-308-6

ISBN 979-8-89041-309-3 (ebook)

Table of Contents

INTRODUCTION

I thought I wasn't going to make it. I just knew I wasn't cut out for this, that the Lord had decided on the wrong person to be a mother and I was somehow being punished for my bad decisions. It can be stressful and overwhelming when raising kids with a partner…even more so when doing it alone. Trying to balance everyday life is enough on its own, so throw in some children, and it will take that "trying" to a whole new level. I had this "dream" of having some sort of balance between raising my kids and keeping my sanity, in addition to growing up myself, but it was only a dream, and as far as I was concerned, morphed into a complete nightmare.

I was pregnant at fifteen and had my daughter a few months shy of my sixteenth birthday. Talk about confusion, sadness, shame, and feelings of defeat. I was all of that and then some. I was still a child myself, working through my own negative self-talk while trying to raise a child that I felt so much shame and resentment toward. Now fast forward, I've ventured into my late twenties/ early thirties with two children, evolving, growing in my faith, going to therapy, and sitting under wise counsel. I am no longer saddened, but still carrying so much shame that I wasn't aware of, and still trying to be intentional about becoming a better mom. I was raised in a large immediate family of ten where I felt love and support on a regular basis, through that love, support, prayer, and counseling I've learned a lot, paired with simple trial and error that came with me raising my children for twenty-nine years. That trial and error was not just me seeing what did/did not work, but also came from listening to my children on what did/did not work.

My hope for you as you dive into this book is that it will not only inspire you to bring a different (not necessarily better) perspective, or spin if you will, to not only how you view and perform within your parenting journey but also to inspire and encourage you to be kind to yourself. You need and deserve the same grace you pour out onto your children. I soon learned that parenting isn't this perfect destination where you finally get everything right, and your children are forever grateful for your sacrifices, but more of a journey of ups and downs where each age is a new stage to learn something different about your children as well as yourself. It's a constant learning of what works and what doesn't, with laughs and better memories as life moves you on.

My Truth

It starts with gratefulness, your perception of a thing. We all know the saying "is the glass half full or half empty," so how you see a thing determines how you'll treat it and whether you will see the fruit of it.

I had an *ah-ha* moment somewhere in the middle of this thing called parenting, possibly in their mid-to-late teenage years, during my prayer time. The Lord showed me that I needed to change my perspective—that my children are a gift from Him. It was really eye-opening for me because while I love my children, I hadn't realized that I had been viewing them as a burden. Yes, I said it, a burden (try not to judge me).

I was carrying around this wound/hurt from my teenage years when I was pregnant. This disappointment and shame was so deep that I couldn't see the forest for the trees. I hadn't forgiven myself for disappointing myself, for letting my parents down, for making my father cry, for disappointing my siblings. I thought I was smarter than that. While my family never verbally told me they were disappointed in me, I felt that they were. I saw the hurt on their faces, and I internalized it.

Not only that, but once my oldest daughter's father started breaking promises, telling her he'd come get her and then leave her at the window waiting for hours, it would literally break my heart. I was having to console, apologize, and come up with excuses for why he didn't show. How do you tell your daughter her father is just no good at such a young age when she'd ask, "Why don't he love me or want me?" Then that became my other cloak of shame, that if I hadn't been disobedient and slept with this horrible guy, she wouldn't be in this pain, so ultimately, it's my fault that she's hurting. I carried that guilt around for years, and it just compounded every time he'd disappoint her, leading to her sitting, waiting at that window or any other area in her life.

The guilt ultimately shaped how I would parent, from a place of hurt, from a place where I reasoned, *okay, I just need to feed, clothe, house, and ensure that holidays, birthdays, and school celebrations are special.* I just need to do what I know to do, so nurturing was not at the top of my list or even on my radar. I was still a child, so I hadn't fully appreciated the nurturing, love, and kindness I received from my parents. So why would it be on my radar? It wasn't. I knew to discipline them because I didn't want to be viewed as a punk. (I couldn't stand disrespectful children—ironic, huh, since I was one.) And I knew to give hugs with affection because that's all we did coming up. You hugged everyone in my family whenever you entered or left a home; we hugged just about everyone in the home.

Anytime they did something wrong, I'd think it was a personal attack, like why don't they see all the things I'm doing or sacrificing to ensure they have what they need, to ensure that they have what little happiness I could provide since I didn't have much money to give them or what I felt like would make them happy? It hurt when I had to say no more than I'd like because I couldn't afford for them to partake in certain family or school activities. I felt like I was failing at this parenting thing (and technically I was) more times than I'd care to admit. On top of that, family would offer to pay for different things and while I allowed it, my prideful thoughts (I didn't realize it was pride back then) would be saying, *you are a charity case; you should be able to do this on your own.* I always felt like I wasn't good enough, and that I had made this huge mistake that would plague me until they were out and able to do for themselves.

But God! As I got closer to the Lord, as my relationship with Him evolved, it went from *why me* to *why not me?* I get to raise these incredibly awesome, intelligent young ladies. I'm honored to be chosen to be their covering. Like really, He chose little ol, attitude filled, damaged me to guide and direct these women. That's huge! They showed me so much about myself—that I was resilient, that I could do this, that I was beautiful, that I was capable. Once my outlook shifted, it opened my heart and mind to receiving the insight the Lord was downloading into me on how to parent His way. It also helped me to listen to my children and really see what their needs were, see how they best felt loved, and opened our communication with each other.

Now let me be clear, although I had this major breakthrough, that does not by any means say that we were lovingly sharing our hearts and minds while bonding and braiding each other's hair. No, we still had moments. Sometimes it was good and sometimes it was bad; we still had to work within this new space. They needed to see, and possibly witness, firsthand that there were some changes happening within their mom, and quite frankly, if it was real. It's a journey in a constant state of evolution. Me learning them in this new light and them learning me, trying our best not to live in the past, convincing ourselves that this is different based on behaviors.

What's your truth, your *ah-ah* moments from your early years in parenting?

_____

_____

_____

_____

_____

In what areas can you change your perspective on parenting?

_____

_____

_____

_____

_____

Transitions

Transition can be scary and uncomfortable, but is very necessary more times than not. That scary lack of comfort affects the child/young adult as well as the parents. The parents are questioning whether their child will make it or discover their niche/passion in life with as little bumps in the road as possible, and the children are doubting if they have what it takes to make it in life, accomplish their goals, and make their parents/guardians proud. The best way I've found to deal with this is through consistent, fervent prayer about what my anxieties and fears are and giving that over to the Lord. Thanking Him in advance for peace and meditating on a verse of comfort. Additionally, I make an intentional choice daily to do better and to check the temperature of how I handled things after each disagreement.

I currently have a sister dealing with this situation; she has a young adult fresh out of high school trying to find his way. He has a job, but outside of that she doesn't quite feel as if he's doing all he can, since after work he comes home and lounges on the couch playing video games. She seems to feel (she didn't verbally state this, just through actions) that consistent nagging about what he's not doing may somehow motivate him to move and try something different. It doesn't. It just makes her son feel as if he can't do anything right and further frustrates/upsets her.

Instead, have a straightforward, candid conversation about his expectations and your expectations, and about how he intends to execute that plan. With that conversation, go in with the mindset that he may not have a plan or an idea. What's the worst that could happen? Invite him/her to come have that conversation with you when they've identified a plan. Let me give you a reminder that it may not be easy, but you support them 100 percent. And whatever questions they have, they should not hesitate to bring them to your attention. Just please remember that there is a large amount of the population that did not find their passion or what they would like to do with their lives until much later in life. Even when one thinks they know after graduation, that can change at least three times before settling/finding what they really enjoy and have a heart for.

When we're frustrated and angry, it's important that we do the work and dissect those emotions to find out why we feel the way we do. It is known that anger stems from fear. So ask; it's imperative to dig deep and find out why/what we're fearful of and address that first before moving forward on a decision or having that discussion with the person we're "angry" with.

What's your current transition, and are you handling it in the best possible way?

_____

_____

_____

_____

_____

Are you angry/hurt/frustrated? If so, why? (Dig deep):

_____

_____

_____

_____

_____

What are you hoping to accomplish? What are you hoping your child/young adult will glean from their interaction with you?

_____

_____

_____

_____

_____

You Won't Have It All Together

Parenting is one of the most gratifying, yet unappreciative, questionable roles on the face of the earth. Most parents (single or not) are still growing and learning themselves while trying to raise another human being successfully, and because we're human, we will mess up. We won't have it all together; there will be plenty of times of questioning decisions you've made, wondering if a decision you've made in your personal life has affected your children, and if so, how.

There will be even more questioning and doubting of your parenting skills when/if you see them making decisions that contradict your beliefs or moral system. If your children stay in a place of bad decisions for a considerable amount of time, this will only compound the guilt. I'm here to tell you this is ALL totally natural! ☺ Regardless of their actions, if you are a reasonable, rational, mature adult, then more than likely you are doing a great job. Even in making mistakes, it is something we can still learn from and do better at the next infraction.

REMINDER! You are not your kids' only influence, so stop taking all the blame on yourself, identify and deal with why, what's your motivation and move forward. The great thing about not having it all together is that there will be continued room for improvement. You will always have the opportunity to re-invent yourself, and failure can also be the catalyst that moves you in a better direction of doing things. Not having it all together also means it's okay to not like your children and to get tired of having to do for them. (No, really, it's okay. ☺) Yes! You can love them. Yes! They are a blessing. Yes! They are your pride and joy, but they will without a doubt get on your LAST nerve and it's okay to admit that. You're human and it can be dang near therapeutic to admit through journaling, venting with your friends/family, or telling God through prayer. However, you do it (in a healthy, non-destructive manner), just do it. Get it out, breathe, and move on to the next situation.

As you move forward to the next stages, good, bad, or indifferent, please be sure to forgive. What do I mean? I'm glad you asked. When we mess up as parents at whatever junction, if we do not forgive ourselves for having placed our children in a negative/bad situation or hurting them, due to our actions, then we can easily find ourselves in a place of forfeiting necessary correction/discipline due to our guilty conscience or constantly beating ourselves up and carrying around the heavy burden of guilt. And yes, sometimes that can happen subconsciously. The purpose of this section is so that you can get ahead of it, or if you happen to be right smack in the middle of it, be intentional about forgiving yourself and move forward.

For years, whenever Denise's father would disappoint her, one thing in particular would be telling her he'd come and pick her up, but he would never show, which left her waiting by the window all night until she fell asleep. It would literally bring me to tears, so I'd start all over with the guilt, blaming myself for choosing that kind of father for her. (It was even hard for me to write this.) How could I be so stupid to allow this to happen? And now that I've caused it, there's no way for me to stop/soothe that pain and disappointment she's feeling. Thanks to my mom, I've never felt it was okay to talk negatively about her father in her presence, but PLEASE believe there were plenty, and I do mean plenty, of times I wanted to tell her "forget about your father—stop asking him because he won't come through for you!" I did not; I allowed her to find out on her own. I had to be intentional about coming to terms with the fact that it happened, they're here, and there's nothing I can do about it at this point but accept it and move on. I had to do all I could to make sure I kept as many promises as possible and to use any opportunity possible to show them how much I loved them.

I think those are the early times, or the training ground, to learn that as a parent you can't fix everything or always have the ability to soothe the hurt your children feel. Looking back now, I wish I'd used that opportunity to have a discussion with her about how to positively channel that disappointment and hurt. I think that was a missed opportunity due to being so focused on my guilt, hurt, and anger around her hurt. That in itself is another place to be intentional in parenting because when it comes to your kids, it can be all emotion and no logical thinking (especially parenting at such a young age). We typically don't make the best decisions when it's all emotion (and that's pretty much any situation). What I've also noticed that helps is consistent mirror motivation. Repeating to myself that I am a good mom! I am doing an awesome job! I will succeed and not fail! My children will be happy and prosperous! I got this! Sometimes we must be our own cheerleader.

Is there any guilt you may be holding on to? If so, what is it and why?

_____

_____

_____

_____

_____

In what ways has it been showing up in your parenting?

_____

_____

_____

_____

_____

What steps can you take to keep guilt from interfering with a more effective form of parenting?

_____

_____

_____

_____

_____

How will you encourage yourself as a parent? (No over-thinking—nothing but cheers! ☺)

_____

_____

_____

_____

_____

From Shame to Freedom

CORRECTION/DISCIPLINE: BE BRAVE

When giving my young adults limitations, I'm reminded that the goal is to help them be a better person and be successful in life. Not just in finances, but emotionally and within relationships, whether personal or professional. They are looking and taking notes from us on how to communicate, resolve conflict, and set boundaries. Yes, it's easy to just say, "she/he is grown, so if they don't want to do right, they can just get out!" However, most times, that solves nothing. Please note that depends on the behaviors; if there's an addiction involved, please seek professional help.

In my current season, I am dealing with my daughter going through a time of doubt, transition, and confusion. While she is over twenty-one, she is still in my care, financially and otherwise. She expressed that she is not happy with my parenting skills, and that she feels I'm disrespectful. We've already had several different conversations regarding this; however, whenever we are halfway through the discussion, she gets so upset that she starts screaming, becoming disrespectful. As you can imagine, at that point she's no longer listening, and to be honest, I am getting somewhat frustrated. Not so much at her, but at the situation itself, because nine times out of ten she won't come down from this without storming out, and nothing has been accomplished.

I would love for us to both walk away feeling loved, understood, and connected (but that would be too much, like right). It finally came down to the last straw for my daughter, where she felt she needed to leave. I expressed that she didn't have to leave; however, she needed to respect me in my house. She continued to leave, even though she had no definitive place to go. I reminded her that I still loved her, that this was still her home, and that she'd always be my baby, and then I had her phone line suspended. As scared and worried as I was for her mental and physical safety, I had to remind myself that this was her choice, and I had to be okay with it. I must love her from a distance. She has since sent me requests for cash, not much, but still a request from the same young lady who was very disrespectful and communicated that she needed me for nothing. I prayed on it and sent a small amount with the message, "I still love you."

Was it hard for me to let go mentally, to take it even further, and suspend her phone line? Yes, absolutely! I cried, prayed, and wondered what was going on with my baby. Then I moved on in peace; not every day peace, but peace for that moment, that day. (Please know that it was a daily struggle.) What helps me daily is staying connected to the Lord through song, sermon, and daily prayer. When I say daily, I literally mean daily. It is the only thing that keeps me in a place of peace. Resting in God during your child's journey, especially when you have a front-row seat to the madness, is one of the hardest things you'll ever have to do as a parent. The point is, you have to set boundaries and some form of discipline. Although that correction will hurt you to your core, it is definitely necessary to help your children move forward and be productive in society. Please believe if they do not have it at home, it will be a rude awakening when they receive it from society; society cares nothing about your kids, so the punishment will be much worse.

As parents, our first thoughts are typically, *how can I fix this? How can I make this better? How can I soothe their hurt?* Contrary to our first reaction/thoughts, sometimes that's not what's need-ed. Sometimes they need to fall; they need to hurt; they need to fail; and while that seems harsh, it really is necessary. I think in our natural need to protect, we forget that experience is the best teacher (as the song says). Think back—a lot of who we are and the wisdom we've acquired is in large part due to our experience with the good, the bad, and the ugly. We don't know what works and what doesn't until we've experienced it. And for some of us, we have that child who just won't listen to reason and typically must find out on their own that if you touch fire, it will burn.

Let's face it, everyone has been there; our parents gave us the best advice, and we were still headstrong on doing it our way because we felt we were grown. We were trying to assert our emancipation—freedom from our parents' direction and "control." Or maybe you're the one who didn't have the best parents, and either mom or dad wasn't around. You were living your life learning as you went along without parental correction, but you still found out what worked and what did not through trial and error—some harsher than others, but you learned.

Let's start asking ourselves how will this correction make them a better adult? What's the intended outcome? We must remember that correction is to correct behavior; it's to make them better. I have found that I am better when I take a moment to get out of my feelings and think about what I want to say and how to say it, depending on the audience, so that I get the best outcome. We must put aside how upset and/or disrespected we feel by their actions, which means letting go of the pride. When we move out of emotion, how do we expect them to react?

Yes, of course I have an example—I'm glad you asked. My daughter was just moving back in with me after being away for some time, so naturally we had to get back acquainted in the form of living together as adults. Mind you, she had free range to move and do as she pleased prior to living with me again, so as you can imagine, we both had our way of doing things. As you'll see throughout the book, I am truly old-school in my parenting, meaning, when you're under my roof I make the rules, and you will respect me with your tone, words, and behaviors.

One night as I was cleaning the kitchen, I asked her to pull out the garbage and place it out front since we have garbage valet that picks up our garbage at the front door. Well, little did I know that this would greatly upset her. It caused her to say to me with attitude, "Why can't my sister take out the garbage?" She stated this didn't make any sense when her sister had been here and was taking out the garbage before she came to stay.

I responded with, "Don't worry about why she can't take it out. I asked you to, so please do so now." She did it, but again, with attitude and mumbling. So my response to that was, "Watch your mouth—be quiet and take out the garbage." Now, of course, anyone who knows me knows this was not said as calmly as it reads. While I wasn't screaming, I wasn't as calm as I could have been. I left it at that, finished the dishes, and went in my room to pray about it because I was fuming and could picture myself doing bodily harm. (Stay with me—I'm just keeping it real.)

After a whole day of calming myself through prayer and re-minding myself that I wanted to change how I discipline, which would directly affect the outcome in how we interact, along with teaching her how to positively resolve conflict, I called her into my room to address the situation. I calmly explained in no uncertain terms that such behavior would not be tolerated in my house again. But I also reminded her that we are a team, that I will always have her back, be open to discussing any frustrations she may have, and that this would not be the first or last time she would be taking out the garbage but that she must do so in a way that was respectful. Mind you, my children were raised doing chores on a daily basis for a week at a time, so I was truly confused at why this upset her so much. It was almost as if we'd just met, but anyhow, I chose not to focus so much on that and focused more on the why and the way it was communicated so that these types of conflict could be handled better going forward, whether with me or anyone else she would have a conflict with in life.

As I observe her discipling my grandbaby, I immediately see the old Monique with the screaming and acting strictly out of emotion and not out of rational thinking. I cringe because that's how she was raised in the first half of her life. While we are not our child's only influence, we do have some influence, so we have to be mindful of what we're passing down; that means being intentional. Like anything else in life, nothing just happens. We must be intentional if we want good relationships, and that includes those with our children. Gone are the days of "do it because I said so." We must also live by example.

Please know that like most things in parenting, this will not be easy. It will take intentional practice, but it can be done. Yes, it is important to even be intentional on the small infractions because those small things not only add up, possibly blowing up into something bigger, but it also prepares you for the bigger issues. (Remember: what's big to you may be small to someone else and vice versa.) Nothing works when we move out of emotion, including discipline/correction.

What long-term outcome do you expect your children to walk away with after your discipline/correction? (Try to dig deeper than just saying, "For them to never do it again."):

_____

_____

_____

_____

_____

What inner work on yourself can be done to improve your responses? Are you the type to respond quickly without thinking? Or do you not respond at all, hoping that if you don't address it, with time it'll just work itself out?

_____

_____

_____

_____

_____

How would your natural response negatively affect your relationship with your children?

_____

_____

_____

_____

How can your intentional response positively affect your relationship with your children?

_____

_____

_____

_____

YOU ARE NOT ALONE

You are NOT alone! It may seem like it and feel like it, but you are not. You are more than capable, or you would not have been blessed with these wonderful children. ☺ Frustration is a hard beast to untangle when raising kids. The frustration can be all-consuming, especially when you see no signs of progress. Here is why I love my faith: even when I don't see it, the Holy Spirit reminds me that He is still in control and provides peace that passes all understanding. I know that sounds preachy or super-spiritual, but that unexplained peace was the only thing that kept me when I was in the thick of the madness—when I couldn't see my way or how things were going to turn around.

I feel like at every stage in life outside of grade school, my children were in the midst of something off the charts, with confusion outside of regular childhood shenanigans. Of course, I felt anger and hurt when my daughter was in and out of trouble all through high school. I was feeling like, *yeah, I'm sick of it*, but also feeling like all teens rebel at some point. Especially given that the youngest never really got in much trouble, so my thoughts there were that everyone's allowed at least one rebellious teenager. Once they hit that eighteen, nineteen range though, all madness broke loose. Both started acting a mess, making bad decisions, hanging with the wrong crowd, with increased marijuana use, trying my patience ☻ more than normal.

Fast forward several years later, and I still feel like they are not moving in the right direction, and when I think they are, I turn around and it's something else. It is, to say the least, EXTREMELY frustrating and a little disappointing; however, it has nothing to do with me or my expectations and everything to do with them being happy, whole, and who God has called them to be. Like most parents, I want the absolute best for my children, and to see them succeed to their fullest potential. When I don't see any steps to it manifesting, I am hurt, frustrated, upset, and confused as to why they are not just moving in the right direction. It seems as if they typically find themselves in some sort of dangerous predicament—guns being pulled on them, fighting, stabbed. This isn't just small trouble we're talking about, and quite naturally, I am worried, scared, ready to fight, AND prepared to go to jail for mine. So not only is dealing with this frustrating, but on top of it all, I'm single and must deal with the emotional fallout on my own. There are no large arms to engulf me, no one to lead me in prayer as I'm wrapped in those arms, no one to bounce around ideas and suggestions that may help my young adults. Now, don't get me wrong. I have a strong faith-based support system that I KEEP on speed dial; however, sometimes it's just not the same since they also have lives to lead.

I'm then reminded that everyone, including me, has their own journey and that it's not about who goes the fastest or who gets the most accomplished in the smallest amount of time. They have their own race to run; they are not in competition with anyone. It will turnaround for the good soon enough, and my only job is to be there, nonjudgmental, loving, encouraging, with a listening ear and open arms.

Being intentional:
What are you currently tired of and frustrated with in this "glorious" life of parenting?

_____

_____

_____

_____

From Shame to Freedom

Are you making it about you? If so, let's change the perspective.

_____

_____

_____

_____

_____

How can you change the perspective? List ways that help you view their negative actions in a positive light.

_____

_____

_____

_____

_____

How are you reacting to the disappointment? Are you judging their actions or are you responding in love? (Try thinking about how you wanted to be treated when you were going through things at that age. *Not how you were treated, but how you wish you were treated.*)

_____

_____

_____

_____

_____

Learn to Rest

To rest in the midst of the stages within their journey is challenging, yet necessary, especially when you have a front-row seat. Rest is taking your concerns and worries to the Lord in prayer, leaving it there, and not allowing what you see to cause you anxiety and stress. The way I have been successful in "leaving it there" (when I am successful) is through daily feeding on the Word of God through song, sermon, or devotional time, and I do mean daily. This regiment has provided me with a peace I cannot explain, while reminding me that their wings work.

In my current season, as I write this book, my oldest (twenty-four years old) lives with me, as well as my bundle of joy, my three-year-old grandbaby. She enjoys smoking the earth and drinks every now and then, so I try to stay in a role of pure guidance, offering the occasional advice on parenting, life, and womanhood. I will literally grind my teeth and clench my fist when catching myself from nagging or repeating something previously discussed.

Now, as you rest and allow your prayers to work, it is incumbent upon us as parents to do right first, even when they don't. To not be petty and to shut down heated arguments and/or disagreement in love. Keep in the forefront that your guidance is still very necessary, even in their young adult stages. Though they probably will not admit it, and may even deny it, they are still in need of and looking to us to be the example.

There have been a number of times my daughters have said something out of pocket, or I felt it was disrespectful, and I have had to LITERALLY stop myself from that first (possibly violent) reaction. (Don't judge me.) I have to stop and think about what

I want the outcome of this interaction to be and if I can use this as a teachable moment or a disciplinary moment of "don't cross me like that again." The bottom line is to resolve the issue or confrontation in a way that builds up and teaches them how to deal with confrontation, not just with others, but with their children as well. Good or bad, it will be passed down to your future generations, so you decide how you want that to look or if it is more important to be right and to save your pride. I'll let you think about that.

List one or two areas that could use some intentionality when having a challenging interaction with your child/young adult:

_____

_____

_____

_____

_____

After a challenging interaction, what does your preferred outcome look like?

_____

_____

_____

_____

_____

What are some ways you can allow them to learn on their own without providing unsolicited advice?

_____

_____

_____

_____

_____

What outcome do you anticipate/expect going into a challenging conversation?

_____

_____

_____

_____

_____

If the outcome wasn't a positive one, how could it have been more beneficial?

_____

_____

_____

_____

_____

If no agreement was met, how can both parties leave at least feeling heard?

_____

_____

_____

_____

_____

Am I Enough?

Do you sometimes think you're not enough, or as if God gave you the wrong children? We will typically ask ourselves this question a handful of times—kudos to you if you haven't, but I know I have throughout my parenting journey. Somewhere around the beginning, and again during those emotional, erratic teenage to young adult years. So here's the reminder (drum roll please): You Are Enough! ☺ You may have asked this question during a long, challenging financial stretch when they really wanted or needed something you were unable to provide. As stated, I don't think it even dawned on me until much later in life that Daddy God gave me these children, these particular children, and that they were something to be cherished. I truly had to change the perspective of feeling as if I was barely making it since they'd been born, you know, glass half full and all that jazz.

The Lord knows what He's doing. Just as He saved us while we were yet sinners, He allowed us to have these children while we may have felt that we're not at our most optimum. It's no surprise that we may question our ability to raise a child, especially when there are challenges. If we're honest, I think we question our ability in a number of ways throughout life's journey. You have everything you need for your children for this stage and age of their lives, make no mistake about it.

I learned that those challenging times were all building my strength, providing wisdom, and stirring up courage along the way. As I matured on my journey, my perspective changed, but as I drew closer to the Lord, my vision became clearer. I began to speak what I wanted to see, not only in my children, but what

I wanted to see in myself. I began to be more intentional about thanking Daddy for providing me with my children, thanking Him for choosing me to cover them. I said, "Lord, there must be something specifically special that You see in me, that You've entrusted these two precious lives under my care." As I became more aware of them as a blessing and not a burden, this really opened me up spiritually, mentally, and emotionally. It allowed me to see my children as God sees me. A flawed individual who needs and desires grace, mercy, and unconditional love. Which, in turn, allowed me to move from a place of love and not discipline.

I became easier to talk to and a much better listener, not the best or perfect listener, just better than I had been previously. When I say a better listener, I don't just mean in the sense of listening while not interrupting. I also mean listening from a space of even after the conversation has ended, I'd step back and really try to see it from their perspective. I was listening from a place of when they are upset/hurt and get slightly disrespectful (and I do mean slightly because the Lord is still working on me), I try to truly dissect what's really behind the emotion. Even again stepping back to pray for discernment and direction.

In these moments, the Lord begins to reveal and remind me that even in our madness we need love, forgiveness, and grace. Even more than that, He begins to reveal to me that as long as I partner with Him, I. Am. Enough.

How can you challenge your parenting in love?

_____

_____

_____

_____

_____

It may be a different area of parenting, but really evaluate your last couple of challenging situations with your children/young adults. Search that and see if you can identify when and where you moved out of emotion and how you can do better. Was it through the lens of love and truly getting a better understanding?

_____

_____

_____

_____

_____

As a parent, in what ways can you give yourself grace?

_____

_____

_____

_____

_____

In what ways can you show your son/daughter grace?

_____

_____

_____

_____

_____

New Levels

When raising kids, each stage is just a new level of flexing those faith muscles. We're still learning. Even with thirty years of experience, I'm still learning and will continue to learn. Each year is a new space with my children never before experienced. Every new year, every new birthday, is a new year for me as their parent. In this year of 2023, my daughters are twenty-six and thirty. I've never parented a thirty-year-old and my twenty-six-year-old is someone totally different from my oldest, which means her year of twenty-six is new to me. New levels, new celebrations, new challenges, a new first with this daughter. This is a new year to learn how to move and to learn how to guide successful young adults strategically.

I want them to not be successful in just money and degrees. I'm not saying that is bad—I want the degree if it's in their journey. My main focus is on how they treat people and in having an authentic, intentional relationship with the Lord. I am concerned with the building of their faith, kindness, and consideration for others.

Every year is a new year for me to learn something new and different as a parent, as a woman. This then raises new situations to evaluate and practice what we've learned in our previous interactions with them. That's why it truly is a journey because as long as we have breath in our bodies, there's opportunity to engage with them in a new way, reasons for being intentional, and the importance of starting intentionally, regardless of the age or stage in the journey.

Reflect on something new in parenting you encountered this year alone.

_____

_____

_____

_____

_____

Was it just an observation or was it a challenging interaction?

_____

_____

_____

_____

_____

If it was challenging, do you think you handled it well?

_____

_____

_____

_____

_____

If not, how could you improve on the next go round?

_____

_____

_____

_____

(Please note that to ask "how could you improve" does not necessarily mean you did something wrong. Improvement could be asking ourselves, *should I have just listened? Should I have asked more questions?* This is simply to challenge our parenting and/or just to encourage our children/young adults to open up more.)

_____

_____

_____

_____

_____

If it was just an observation, what were the *ah-ha* moments (if any)?

_____

_____

_____

_____

_____

Necessary Partnerships

Sometimes it's the simplest messages that we know to be true that we cannot get down in our spirit. Messages like, *you're only human, it takes a village, people make mistakes*. Stop beating yourself up when you can't make it to all of your children's events, award assemblies, and recognitions. Partner with the Lord so that He may transform how you see yourself, and partner with friends and/or family that have your best interest at heart for support. If you're lacking family and friends, then utilize what you have, be intentional about attending or volunteering at your child's school. Being intentional in this way puts you in a position to meet other parents and build a community for that support. When trying to find some sliver of balance in making it to events, assemblies, trips, and volunteering, remember that you're only human. Give more attention to the events/engagements that you did make by focusing on when you are there for them. It's hard with one child and you're the only active provider, so double or triple that when you have more than one. You cannot make it to every event, be a personal chauffeur, AND "bring home the bread" regularly. You must give yourself some grace (as Daddy does ☺). Now, of course, this shouldn't be a chronic situation of missing school events. We should always look for a better way to move so that there's some sort of balance. See how we can rotate in at least one of every event within a certain amount of time.

The same applies to our conversations and/or disciplinary tactics. We won't always get it right, so just be intentional about changing things up the next go round, then continue to evolve in that space. Just because you still may be making mistakes in your relationship with your child/young adult, and just because what you see does not look like the vision you see in your head, does not mean you are failing as a parent. Remember, just like life, this process is a journey, NOT a destination. I can't stress the journey part enough. You both are constantly growing and evolving, learning new things about yourself on a regular basis.

I also relate this to a relationship or marriage in which you and your partner/friend are constantly progressing. I believe we must grow more and adapt to each other. At any point that one of the partners in the relationship decides to choose not to accept this change/growth/evolution that they see in their partner, the sooner that relationship eventually comes to a screeching halt. Now, please believe this does not apply to when a relationship becomes abusive, toxic, or unhealthy. The bottom line is non-movement and non-adaptability keep us stagnate in life.

One way I've adapted to work on growth and staying flexible is "calling myself on the carpet," being self-aware, being intentional about thinking through not only my actions, but my thoughts that led me to that action. *Was I upset, and if so, why was I upset? Why is it that what they did led me to be upset? What was I afraid of? Did I handle it correctly/effectively? Was he/she able to get some sort of insight to ponder on later?" What were some other ways I could've handled it?* You can do this by either writing the questions down or mulling over it in your thoughts. Let's be clear, I don't successfully achieve this in all my interactions with my children, only those that made a loud noise resulting in storming off, hurt feelings or if I've walked away thinking there may have been a huge disconnect in our understanding or perception.

Being self-aware is one of THE best tools to have in your arsenal. Using that tool means having the ability to face and deal with some ugly things either in your past or present. It means being very honest with who you are and the why—full transparency. Transparency with yourself can take your relationships from surviving to thriving and facilitates your child into transparency.

We all have something. The sooner we start digging deeper the better off we'll be.

One of the best partnerships I've entered into was the one with my Lord and Savior, Jesus Christ. The freedom and peace that comes with and continues throughout our relationship is unmatched. Some days I don't even have the words to describe how He is a very present help in the time of trouble. How freeing it is to be able to move in a space of uncertainty and not be moved by the circumstance. To not know how things are going to work out but to know that you know that the Lord has already worked it out in your favor. I only wish I'd had this revelation early on in my walk; it would've saved me years of extended worry and stress. The deal is to build a relationship, not religion. This building is similar to how we build earthly relationships, through spending time and intentionality. To be so consumed in His Word and time with Him that when the heat of life is turned up, you can walk out and not even smell like smoke.

Who's your village and why?

_____

_____

_____

_____

_____

How are you practicing your growth and adaptability as a parent?

_____

_____

_____

_____

_____

What outcome did you envision? If that wasn't the outcome in reality and/or there was no resolution, how could the outcome have been more beneficial?

_____

_____

_____

_____

List some things you could've done differently and put them into practice.

_____

_____

_____

_____

Loving Them Through It

Showing love through what we think is madness isn't always easy. Not allowing your "I don't agree" feelings to show through actions or facial expressions is also not the easiest…at least for me it wasn't. As our children stumble and fall throughout their journey, it is imperative that we are intentional with displaying love for them on a consistent and regular basis. My daughter is living an alternative lifestyle that I do not agree with; I don't condone it. It was truly a challenge for me, not so much to show love, but showing love that she could feel. Being in touch with how she feels most loved. Let me tell you, this was not the easiest, especially since her communication skills aren't quite polished yet. So it was basically trial and error, just as it is in all aspects of parenting. It typically didn't come up until she was extremely frustrated or mad, so now I had to be creative in not only finding out how to flow in peace with her, but also how to get her to slow down, breathe, and articulate what she was feeling.

When I tell you it's taxing as ever on your mental and emotional well-being, I mean that. Dealing with her in the midst of those mood swings makes me want to throw up my hands and say forget it. Especially around the age of twenty-one when she really didn't stay with me. But GOD! It's important to me that she gets it right, and when I say right, I'm not speaking of her lifestyle; that's between her and God. I'm referring to communication, how to express her anger, frustration or hurt without shutting down and/or blowing up.

My bottom-line is to love her as Christ loves me, and that's unconditionally. As long as she keeps that door open, I'll walk through it EVERY time. She's battling with a lot on the inside and dealing with hurt that she isn't ready to address yet. Since she isn't ready, I'm giving her all the grace she can possibly stand while reminding her that I love her. Now don't get me wrong, I still have to put my foot down and set up boundaries when she gets disrespectful or out of hand. Even with those boundaries up, whether it's through a call, text, or social media messenger, I remind her that she is still one of my heartbeats and that I will never give up on her. I love her with all the love of Jesus Christ. It's interesting though. I look at age and experience throughout this journey and remember thinking somewhere in my thirties that *I get this; I've matured so much as a parent.* I have matured; however, it was in those last few years of my thirties/early forties that I truly saw growth, wisdom, and maturity.

I recall she was having one of her loud, emotional outbursts, yelling, storming around grabbing her things out of her room, screaming that she was leaving/moving out with a friend that was no good for her. Being very disrespectful; however, all through that outburst, while I was certainly hurt, all I could feel was sadness and pain that she was so hurt/damaged inside that she was going through this. One, because I knew what she was battling and what was hurting her. Two, because this was not typical behavior, at least not to this extent. In that moment, the fact that I was hurting for her and not mad at her for the disrespect showed me I had grown.. Like for real, no ounce of anger, just pure hurt. It hurt me that she was going through so much and didn't know the proper way to express it before it got out of hand. She left, I went in my room, cried, and fell on my face before the Lord, praying for her safety and healing.

As you probably guessed, she called crying, asking to come back home a couple weeks later. I didn't fuss about how, or why, or her behavior when she left. I simply said, "Yes, what do you need?" I bought a bus ticket and had my baby home the next day. Simply put…Grace.

Think about your last unpleasant encounter with your child/
children/young adult. How could you have applied grace?

_____

_____

_____

_____

_____

Share a situation when grace wasn't used. How could you have
applied it? Why do you think it was not applied (i.e emotion,
pride, etc.)?

_____

_____

_____

_____

_____

CREATING BOUNDARIES

Creating boundaries with your children can be challenging; we can get so caught up in our everyday dance that we tend to forget to continue to set those boundaries along the way. So what you may have put in place for your child as an understanding early on changes as they become preteens, as they become full-on teenagers, and then as young adults. This happens quite naturally because your dynamics change within the relationship. With that, then it's important to continue setting new boundaries with every new phase we encounter in life.

Growing up, my children have ALWAYS had chores, whether it was washing dishes, cleaning the living area, or washing clothes. When they were as young as eight years old, I would take them with me to the laundromat and they'd help sort, load, and pour the soap. As they got older, they graduated to doing a full week of cleaning the kitchen while the other would have a full week of cleaning the living and dining room, then they'd switch and alternate weeks. They would also have to collectively keep their rooms clean. Now, one would think that having grown up completing chores on a regular basis, this would be a given responsibility as they reached their late teens and into adulthood.

Now fast forward, as they became young adults, they were going back and forth from staying with me in different phases and stages. Leaving, staying with others for six months to a year or so, and then living with me again—basically a revolving door. Now, while they have had to clean basically their entire life while growing up, here they are early to mid-twenties, and I have to have multiple conversations with grown folks about cleaning the house regularly when they're home. I didn't, I'm sure like most, think that deeply or intentionally about setting the precedence every time they returned home, which led me to me just telling them on the fly to clean, from leaving text messages to voice messages as reminders to remember to clean. I'm sure it was because we had our own lives still moving on with schooling, jobs, friends…living life, so it wasn't at the top of my list of things to address— until it was. My thoughts and hopes were, *okay, they're staying here, they know my expectations around cleaning since that's how they were raised.* Sooooo, that would equate to cleaning up when you're home, whether it's what you messed up or you just see the need.

Boy, was I mistaken. Now weeks or months have passed by, and I'm still sending side reminder messages about cleaning. Once I caught them in the house together, then I had to have that conversation, expressing the importance of cleaning up and continuing to clean, ESPECIALLY when you are not paying rent or any major bills. That's their way of not only "earning their keep" but also showing their appreciation to the person who was housing them. Needless to say, I was given push back from both of them. One even had the nerve to say that since she is paying one bill (yes, one bill), her sister, who is not paying, should be responsible for the cleaning. Not to mention, they both had a child; yeah, I know, crazy right.

My thought was, *they're adults so I'm going to treat them as such and give them the benefit of the doubt.* I assumed I could just tell them, "Hey, clean this or clean that," and they'd pick up on it and run with it. It was good to have that assumption; however, I noticed the more I gave them leeway, the more things stayed the same, and now I found myself doing most of the cleaning in the common spaces. Now I had to sit them both down and have that come-to-Jesus conversation, stating that I would not continue to go back and forth with them on this, reminding them that you can't sleep anywhere that you don't clean/contribute to the household. Either they could decide they'll clean up here or move somewhere else, but they can't do both. They can't stay here and decide they're not going to clean. With that, I gave them a deadline, which was two days (and that two days was generous) to decide if they were going to stay under my roof and contribute or if they were going to move.

Often, it serves us better to simply think about the best way to handle things before addressing something that could be a potential situation. Most times you don't know that it's a bigger situation until you're in the thick of it. However, I realized going forward that I'm going to address a situation as soon as I have to repeat myself that first time. When I allow it to linger in hopes that they'll get it or simply because I don't feel like addressing it, then by the time I do address the situation, I have so much frustration and built-up hostility that I blow up. Now I'm dealing with it out of pure emotions, and typically nothing is handled well when our emotions take over. I can also run the risk of tension between us all that will be felt throughout the home, becoming passive aggressive because I have not addressed or set boundaries/ground rules. Remembering that my goal is to not only address a problem, but to address it in a way that mirrors how adults should handle conflict, as well as maintaining a good relationship with my children. Boundaries set the tone for healthy relationships across the board.

What boundaries have you set that you've found helpful?

_____

_____

_____

_____

_____

Are boundaries something you'd like to have in place but haven't done so yet? If so, why do you think you haven't?

_____

_____

_____

_____

_____

Think about it, what are some areas in your life or within your home that could use some healthy boundaries?

_____

_____

_____

_____

_____

Conclusion

Where are we now? Living life. Still learning, still exploring, evolving. Is it perfect? Do we have all the answers? You've guessed it…nope, but we're evolving in a way where we can have good, meaningful conversations and be respectful at the same time. This also doesn't mean that I still don't struggle from time to time with wondering if my children will be okay or if we'll make it another day without "killing" each other. What this does mean is that every day that we wake up is a new day for a new outlook on life, a new outlook on our relationship and a new day to change it up if yesterday didn't go as planned. Remember, every day that you and your children have breath in your bodies is a day to start over.

My prayer is that you have identified your truth while viewing your parenting from a new perspective. I hope that you've pulled back some layers on the *why* for responses within these transitions, you've either continued or will start to encourage yourself with grace and without shame. Be brave, it is work that can be rewarding…maybe not after every win (or what you'd see as a win) but it is rewarding, again it's about your perception of a thing.

Embrace the changes and "rest." I believe that eventually the goal for all parents is to raise kind, productive, loving, respectful, and ambitious members of society. (For me, members of God's kingdom.) I want my children to also thrive in their journey with His shalom peace, His rest, sanity, respect, and appreciation for His grace and mercy. It is my prayer that my story has helped you start or continue on in your journey with a new frame of mind. You are not alone! You are enough! Find your village, support, and encouragement where you are or within one of my cafés with other parents, either online or in person.

You've got this!